Mistakes I made My First 5 Years in Business (and How You Can Avoid Them)

Elizabeth K. Fischer

Monarch Tree Publishing

Eau Claire, Wisconsin

Mistakes I Made My First Five Years in Business (and How You Can Avoid Them).

Published by Monarch Tree Publishing, P. O. Box 387, Eau Claire, Wisconsin 54702-0387. (888) 895-7166.
First printing 2002.

The clients, circumstances, and experiences cited in this publication represent a blend of many businesses and companies that I have advised during my first five years as a marketing consultant. It is not my intent to identify or reveal individuals, specific businesses, trade secrets, or client confidences. Rather, my intent is to show the mistakes I made my first five years in business in hopes that others will not make these same mistakes.

ISBN 0-9721255-1-5

Library of Congress Control Number: 2002112160

Attention organizations and educational institutions:
Quantity discounts are available on bulk purchases of this book for educational purposes or fund raising. For information, please contact Monarch Tree Publishing, P. O. Box 387, Eau Claire, Wisconsin 54702-0387. (888) 895-7166. Fax: (715) 874-6766. www.monarchtreepublishing.com

Dedicated to SRL for listening to all my mistakes my first five years in business. She knows that this could have been a three volume set, rather than fourteen chapters. Some mistakes are better left unsaid since they will serve no useful purpose in telling.

Acknowledgements

Thank you to Sharon R. Lowry for painstakingly editing this book. Her hours of effort have improved the communication of my ideas and greatly enhanced the text.

Thank you also to Jill Olsen for the attention-getting cover, for the logo, and for all the talent and enthusiasm that she has poured into this project.

Thank you to my success team for their encouragement and feedback chapter by chapter.

Contents

Preface

With the current boom in new small business, which does not appear to be slowing down, many books giving advice are on the market about starting and running your own small business. All have something to say, and most have advice nuggets that will make and/or save you money.

So who needs another book on running your own small business?

I read many of the books on starting my own small business, and then proceeded to make many of the mistakes against which they cautioned.....plus a few more. My hope for you is that if I share some of my mistakes, it may help you avoid them. Fortunately, I have survived my mistakes. I hope you do, too.

Come along and review with me some of the mistakes from which I learned how to successfully run a small business.

My Rule List

After five years in business, I realized that certain situations created an unprofitable, stressful business for me. These situations kept me from achieving my dreams. From these, I made a list of "rules" to help myself avoid these situations in the future.

My rule list is as follows:

Do not work with committees.

Work with situations that have only one person who makes the decision rather than deal with a manager and a general manager, both of whom may have input into the decision.

Work with people who can and do make decisions.

Treat all friends as you would strangers in business dealings.

Listen to my "gut feelings." If a situation doesn't feel right, don't do it.

Always have an agreement signed before I begin work.

Price the project fairly for myself and for the client.

Do not "give away" ideas to clients to get work from them. Ideas are what I have to sell. If I give them away, I have nothing to sell.

Value myself and my work at the level that I want others to value me.

The book you are about to read will explain the mistakes that I made from which I developed these rules. As you read the book and examine your business, make a list of your own rules. Post them where you can review them frequently and live by them. Your rules will increase your business's profitability.

1
How I Began My Business

Like so many entrepreneurs, I fled from the restrictive corporate world to begin my business. At the time I worked for a TV station as a sales representative. Having always worked hard and enjoyed doing so, I had built my account list up to be the top local list at the station. Management didn't like the size of my list because it meant that I could make more than some managers, which was a no-no in that company.

After I had fought hard with two general sales managers to keep my list intact, a new general sales manager arrived from corporate headquarters. One of his top priorities was to cut my account list. He hired a new representative was hired and gave him one-fourth of my list. I was told that if I ever billed over a certain amount again, I would have more accounts taken away from my list. When I inquired as to my incentive to increase sales, I was told that they would build that into my compensation plan. Yeah, right!

This situation left me with three options. The first was to change the way I work. Stop working so hard. Don't go out after new accounts. Don't try to get more business from current accounts. In essence, change myself and the core of who I was. I concluded that I liked who I was and didn't want to change. I passed on the first option.

The second option was to keep on working the way I had been working, despite the new rules. However, when my account list grew to the point that more accounts would be taken away from me, I would have gotten very upset. I would have looked at myself in the mirror and seen a fool. After all, management had warned me, hadn't they? I would have then proceeded to develop an irreconcilable bad attitude. This option wasn't a long term solution, either.

The third option was to follow my dream of having my own business. I had dreamed of controlling my time and not having management dictate my income. At that point in time, my financial situation was such that I could take the chance of starting my own business. Thus, I decided to take the plunge and go into business for myself. I determined that if the business was not profitable, what was the worst that could happen? I could always go back to working for someone else.

However, I didn't immediately turn in my resignation and open my business the next day.

Read about entrepreneurs

First, I read a book or two on opening my own business. As I read these books, I realized that I fit the profile of an entrepreneur. I took initiative, was self-motivated, liked to work by myself, was innovative, was willing to risk, and had several other attitudes and characteristics recommended for entrepreneurial success. As I read, I began to realize why I had always felt out of place in the corporate world. Like most entrepreneurs, I didn't fit the corporate mold. The idea of opening my own business became more and more appealing as I read these books.

Decided what business

Next, I thought about what business to open. The easiest transition was a business in which I could work with the clients that I had worked with as a TV sales representative. The advertising and marketing business was also my area of expertise. Consequently, the idea of opening an advertising agency was interesting to me. However, unlike similar cities its size, Eau Claire did not have a business climate that supported many advertising agencies. A couple agencies had done well, but many had not stayed in business.

Why?

Researched my business

I did research on this question by asking several of my clients what they thought about advertising agencies. All of them had the same answer. They felt that advertising agencies took control and did not listen to what they, the customers, wanted. They also felt that advertising agencies cost too much. In their eyes, an advertising agency would be expensive because of its fees. In addition, their business's spending for advertising would be out of control because it would be in the hands of the advertising agency.

I realized from this research that business people were searching for guidance and advice on their marketing. Once they received this advice, they could implement much of their own marketing with the assistance of whatever media that they were using. In some instances, business people wanted more help than just the initial advice, but in general, they just needed to know what to do.

Created business plan

From this information, I developed a business plan of a marketing consulting business. Calling my business marketing consulting served two purposes. One, it aptly described what I was doing. I was consulting with clients to help them decide what to do with their marketing. Two, no business in the Eau Claire area had ever called itself a marketing consultant before, so when I did so, I got questioned, "What is a marketing consultant?" This, of course, was a perfect opening to describe my business in terms that did not fit the area's advertising agency paradigm. It gave me an opportunity to set my business apart. It gave me a chance to shape opinions of what my business did.

Set a time table

Now that I knew what business I was starting, I set a time table for getting it off the ground. The date was March, 1994. I decided to turn in my resignation in late June with two weeks' notice so that I was finished with my job after the first week in July, 1994. This time frame gave me time to finalize my business plan, get my business cards and stationery developed and printed, and buy equipment. Basically, it gave me time to do what I needed to do to get my business started. From a financial point of view, this time table enabled me to finish the second quarter of billing, which was the second strongest quarter of the year. This yielded a great deal of revenue to me. It also enabled me to get all of my July billing set so that when I left in early July, I already had made my commissions for the entire month. I followed this time table and, consequently, was able to start my business with cash in my pocket.

During my advertising sales career, I had seen many businesses that had failed because they had not planned and capitalized well at their start. Therefore, I planned and capitalized so that I would avoid those pitfalls. It paid off, because I *did* avoid those pitfalls. There were other pitfalls, however, that I did not avoid. Some, such as billing, I had read about, but it took experiencing billing to fully appreciate its pitfalls. Others, such as losing focus or giving my time and services for free, had not been discussed in any book or article that I had read.

Mistakes happen-recognize them

So, despite my attempts to avoid pitfalls, or mistakes, I proceeded to make them. Fortunately, I have recognized my mistakes, learned from them, and survived them, although I did not acknowledge these mistakes the first time I made them. All of these mistakes happened to me more than once. Many happened several times. In fact, some of these mistakes I still struggle with today because the opportunities to make these mistakes present themselves everyday. Hence, I must be vigilant to remember my mistakes and their lessons. Otherwise, it's easy to repeat them.

Since writing this book, I've decided that rereading this book regularly may help remind me of these mistakes, help me recognize them quickly, and help me avoid repeating them.

That, however, was not my original reason for writing this book. I wrote this book to help you recognize these mistakes, hopefully before, but if not before, at least *when* you make them the first time. In addition to describing my mistakes, I will also give you my solutions to them. While mine are not the only ways of handling these mistakes, the solutions have worked for me, and I hope you will find them of use to you, too.

2
Friends...Love 'em and Leave 'em Alone

When I started my business, I found it was an easy transition to work with the clients I had had as a television sales representative. Several of the ones that I had asked for feedback when I was researching the business asked after the research interview session to have me handle their marketing when my business started. Of course, just as you would do, I took the business. When you are in great trepidation about income and someone asks you to work with them, you do not hesitate; you eagerly say yes, right?

I learned from this experience not to work with friends.

You see, many of these clients had become my friends through our business association while I was a TV sales representative. These clients were not friends in terms of socializing, but friends in terms in the sense that I was someone on whom they could rely for help in their marketing whenever they needed advice. These client friends were accustomed to getting "free" advice and extras done for them when I was a TV sales representative. At that position, I could justify these extras as the customer service part of my job. As an owner of my own business, it was a different matter.

Extras affect revenue

Do you see where this is leading? At the time, I didn't. I was accustomed to operating by giving extras. While I realized that in my own business, I needed to make money from my advice, I didn't realize how much these extras could deduct from my business's revenue. I also didn't realize that how client friends viewed my expertise would affect my dealings with them. Their views and their expectations of extras became a stumbling block for my business. For a while, I was unaware of what was happening. After awareness dawned, I thoroughly reviewed the situation in my mind several times to understand it. My review yielded three points.

How client friends saw me

First of all, I was in the steep part of a learning curve in my new business. Some client friends saw me only for what they knew I could do and did not fully trust my abilities in other areas. They viewed me as an expert in TV, but not competent in other media, such as print. In one instance, a client friend hired me to help with a print piece. I did the layout, researched the mailing list, found the mail house, and held overall responsibility for getting the piece printed and distributed. Throughout the entire project, my client friend doubled-checked decisions, almost every one it seemed, with anyone else. By anyone, I don't mean other people in the printing or marketing field, but employees, friends, and business people who had no marketing expertise. Frustratingly, it felt to me that *any* person's opinion was as valuable as mine to this client friend, which translated into mistrust to me. This mistrust from a client friend was more upsetting than mistrust from a stranger. My resulting upset affected not only the work I was doing with that client friend, but my work with other clients as well.

On the other end of the spectrum, other client friends never questioned my expertise and expected me to operate as if I had been doing all facets of marketing for years. An example of this occurred with the first newspaper ad which I created that contained a picture. The ad was furnished to the newspaper camera ready as a hard copy on paper, printed by a laser printer. This was before zip disks or CDs, which is hard to remember but, really, was not *that* many years ago. While the ad looked sharp on paper to myself and to the client, it printed very darkly in the newspaper because it was generated by a laser printer. I found this out after the ad was printed, when the ad looked disappointingly dark in the newspaper. Neither myself nor the client had had this experience before. No one at the newspaper told me that laser printed pictures darken in newsprint until *after* the publication of the ad, when I inquired as to the picture's darkness. This was a learning experience for all concerned, especially me. Although my client accepted the explanation of what had happened and never complained, the experience left me feeling that I had let my client down.

Both client friends' attitudes, that of underlying mistrust and that of total confidence, taught me lessons. On the one hand, I was struggling to show that I knew what I needed to know. On the other, I was scrambling for answers when I didn't, all the while maintaining a calm facade to clients. This vacillation was time-consuming and emotionally draining.

Secondarily, because as a TV sales representative I had always done extra for my clients, they continued to expect the same treatment. The problem was that as a TV sales representative I was being paid to keep the clients as customers, and as an independent businesswoman the clients needed to pay me for this treatment, which, of course, they had never done before. In addition, I was struggling within myself to set "fair" prices that I thought the clients would pay.

Change client expectations?

It may be hard to teach an old dog new tricks, but it is even more difficult to change well-entrenched client expectations. I did not have the security, experience, or courage to sit down and discuss their expectations with my clients. So I was a part of the problem, too. I was accustomed to delivering more than expected and did not want to change that. The difficulty was how could I give time-consuming service and still have enough time to run a profitable business? As you may have guessed, I sacrificed a great deal of personal time as well as profit as I worked through the quandary.

Thirdly, it was very easy for client friends to call and ask for something to be done that was not in our agreement. And I would honor their request, without charging for the additional work. You see, our agreement was vague and verbal because I was apprehensive about setting limits on paper with these client friends. They had never had limits, either verbal or written, from me before! Being the friend that I was, I usually followed through on the request without thinking that a modification should be made in the verbal agreement. When I did give that thought, I was too concerned about treading on the toes of our friendship to mention it. I feared losing a friend, and a client, by doing so.

When not to deal with family and friends

Friendship makes it difficult to do business and be fair to both parties. Most of the time neither side deliberately sets out to take more from the other, but it happens nonetheless. When you are starting a business or changing what you do in a business, all the uncertainty and newness that you face places you in a very vulnerable position. This is a particularly critical time not to deal with friends, especially client friends you know from your former work. You need time to get established with people who take you at face value, not those who have preconceived notions of what you do and who you are. Friends can unwittingly put you in a box by their attitudes toward you and force you to stay there. Their expectations of you help form *your* opinion of *your* work, and you get caught in a vicious cycle of first keeping them happy, then breaking out to do the work you want to do with new clients, all the while keeping faith in yourself and your abilities in the process.

This is unprofitable and emotionally draining.

After a few years of struggling with this issue and feeling frustrated with myself, my friends, and the situation, I realized that I needed to do business with strangers. The strangers, or people who hadn't worked with me in my TV sales representative career, did not have preconceived notions of my abilities and viewed me as an expert in my field.

The fact that strangers take you for the expert you say you are is wonderful. It's up to you to actually be that expert and merit their trust.

I found a freedom and an exhilaration in working with these strangers that I hadn't found with friends and, after much introspection, came to the realization that working with friends is not profitable for either party.

In the years since that realization, if a friend contacts me, I mentally deal with that person as if he or she is a stranger. I quote a fee up front, have a contract signed, and do not do extra unless it is added to the contract. Do I still give a friend free advice at times? Yes, and, as I do with everyone, I limit that advice, telling that person when I do so that "this is a freebie."

Treat friends as strangers

Therefore, keep in touch with your friends, but don't work with them unless you treat them like strangers. One side will get cheated or feel like it has been, and it will probably be you. Friends....love 'em and leave 'em alone...in your business, that is.

3

Losing Focus

When you have your own business, the temptation to lose focus is constant.

Very often, you get tempted to drop your business in favor of working for someone else. The tantalizing finger of not having to shoulder the responsibility of your business and of being assured of a paycheck beckons you. It can be difficult not to answer. Some business owners do go back to working for someone else, although seldom for long. If you have your own business because you want to control your time and your destiny, handing this control back to someone else is not satisfying. In the midst of a money crisis or a deadline, dumping those responsibilities onto someone else may seem appealing, but what you give up along with those responsibilities is too much to sacrifice. What you give up is control.

Who has control

Let's face it. If you are in business for yourself, one of your principal reasons for being in business is control. That is also why it is difficult for a business person to work for someone else. The business person wants to be in control, which may not jive with "a boss" wanting to be in control. A year or so after I started my business, one of my clients from my television days called me and asked me to make a play for their marketing position. He said they were outsourcing the job and that it would not be a full-time position. For a struggling new business person such as myself, this seemed a great opportunity. So I created a campaign and traveled ninety miles to present it. They were quite impressed and offered me the work. There was just one catch, however. My friend, who worked in the organization and had invited me, was trying to convince the two owners to outsource the position. The owners were not convinced and did not feel comfortable with the outsourcing. They wanted the person in the position to work out of their office and under their noses. My acceptance of the position meant ditching my business and moving my residence. I didn't want to do either and declined the offer.

Declining wasn't easy, though. I had to sort out my priorities and think through what I really wanted in order to realize that I didn't want the offer.

What makes you lose focus

Lack of established priorities and lack of time to think contribute to losing focus on a daily basis. I find myself, and frequently hear other business people, saying, "I'm having trouble focusing." Have you felt this way? This usually happens when you are going along day to day caught up in the current of your business and doing what needs to be done. You are so busy working in a rut that you don't take the time to check out what rut you are working in. Was this the rut you intended to be in? Will it take you where you want to go? If you have lost focus, you probably don't know.

When I lose focus, I find that no matter what I do, I have a feeling of not being done. I feel confused. I feel vaguely anxious, and I don't know why. I feel pulled in several directions. I feel that I am not accomplishing anything. I feel dissatisfied. I feel aimless and adrift.

Losing focus is unsettling.

It happens when I haven't set priorities or I have gotten away from following the priorities that I had set.

Recently, I reread the classic book, Think and Grow Rich by Napoleon Hill. I originally read it several years ago, and thoroughly enjoyed it. I cannot say, however, that I followed his instructions, which were to set priorities or goals, put them in writing, and read them aloud twice daily, visualizing their achievement. When I recently read Think and Grow Rich, I was struck by how helpful following those instructions might be. I, like many people, perhaps like you, had vague goals that I had never committed to paper.

One of these goals was writing this book. I had mentioned the idea to a few people and talked about it with colleagues but had never written down that I would actually do it. After rereading Think and Grow Rich, I decided to try Napoleon's suggestion. I sat down and thought through my priorities and goals. Wow! That took some time! Figuring out what I really wanted did take time. I found that I had not been focusing on profitable projects and streams of income. I found that I had been drifting along in the current of my rut, taking whatever business came my way, and not pursuing my goals. It became very apparent to me why I was losing focus.

What do you *really* want?

I decided my goal was to be financially free by creating assets that generate income without my direct, continuous involvement. While I love marketing consulting, doing only that everyday would not accomplish this goal. Writing a book about what I learned would become an asset which could contribute toward financial freedom. So I wrote down another goal of writing this book within two months and getting it published a couple months after that. Clearly stating this goal with dates attached made the goal a directive. It seemed real. Then reading that goal daily focused my mind like a heat-seeking missile.

I cannot believe how focused my attention has

become since following Napoleon's instructions. I have clarity of thought. I am getting not only this book, but also a great many other goals accomplished. I am excited about my work and, more importantly, about my direction. I have also been enormously helped by my weekly success team's keeping me on track by asking about the book as well as giving me feedback on the chapters I have written.

In retrospect, it seems easy to understand why I lost focus. I had none. If I did not know what I was focusing on, how could I focus on it? If I did not know where I was going, any road would get me there! I hadn't taken the time to think through, and then to write down, where I was going. No wonder I felt vaguely anxious. I was meandering through my daily business without a clear path. Without goals, I was like a ship on the ocean without a charted course to my destination. It didn't matter if I had a flashy compass. New sails wouldn't help. A great crew's talents might be underutilized. Without clearly written goals, I would continue to be aimlessly adrift in a sea of business opportunities.

Lately, I make particular note of other business people who complain of losing focus. I haven't quizzed them on this, but in conversation it appears that, just as I have experienced, they have not thought through and written down their goals, either.

Think about this for just a minute. If you haven't consciously established your focus, how can you focus on it?

Do you have a focus? What *is* your focus?

Make an appointment with yourself

If you cannot read the answer to these questions from your written goals, make an appointment with yourself right now to think through your goals. Give yourself plenty of time for your appointment. I took hours. Ask yourself, “What do I want?” When you know, write your goals down. Make them clear. Attach dates. Quantify them by stating your goals in terms that are measurable. Then, as Napoleon instructs, read them daily. If you follow through on this, you will be amazed at what you accomplish.

Most importantly, you will not complain of losing focus because you will *have* a focus.

This book is testament that setting, writing down, and daily reviewing your goals works. After all, you are holding one of my focused goals in your hands, aren’t you?

4

FREE??

Small business people have many opportunities to do business for free. Some are legitimate promotional opportunities. Some are charitable giveaways. And some are totally unnecessary.

Unnecessary freebies

Small business people give away these totally unnecessary freebies because we have a mindset that we must to do so to get business. At a recent meeting of entrepreneurial business women that I attended, one of the business owners commented, "As small businesses, we must give away a great deal of business." Must we?

Why?

When I started my business, I had difficulty giving clients proposals. I felt that in the proposal I should give them an example of what I could do for them. In other words, I should give them an idea for their marketing to demonstrate my competence. I wanted to give them a sample of what I could do. I wanted to "wow" them. In doing proposals this way, I ran the risk of the clients' using my ideas as a freebie and not paying me for them. After all, I had put these ideas in a proposal with no strings attached.

Luckily, I did business mostly with people I knew and trusted, so that ideas taken without payment did not happen to me, at least of which I was aware. However, several years into my business, I made a proposal to a grocery store whose owners did take my idea and not pay me for it. Between our initial meeting and the meeting at which I gave the store owners a proposal, I did some research on the store's business. One of my conclusions from my research was that the store's competition all used a personal name, whether first or last, such as Fred's Foods or George's IGA. In my proposal I suggested that the store change its name to include the store owners' name, so that the community could also call this store by a personal name, which would put the store on a more even footing with its competition. Consumers in that area liked to do business with stores that sounded like they were run by the consumers' neighbors. Thus, incorporating the owners' name into the store's name would make the store more attractive to consumers. Well, the store owners didn't hire me, but they did take my freebie idea and change the name of the store to include the owners' name. A summer later I had occasion multiple times to drive by a sign the owners had erected on a busy highway, which, of course, used the new store name that I had suggested. Every time I passed that sign I was painfully reminded of my freebie to the store and its owners.

Don't giveaway ideas

This experience taught me not to give ideas away in my proposals. I finally internalized what I had been trying to teach myself for years: What I have to sell is ideas. If I give these ideas away in my proposals or in conversation before I have the work, I run the risk of having the client use the idea without paying me for it. I couldn't afford to have a business in which I gave away what generated revenue for me.

I started doing proposals that did not include ideas, but instead reviewed the client's situation and then stated what my actions would be to help the client. I stopped putting any sampling of ideas in my proposals at all, at least with a client I hadn't worked with previously. There are times, yet, when I give an idea to ongoing clients prior to our having an agreement. Of course, they always pay me for it. Thus, it is not a freebie.

However, I still must resist the temptation to give ideas away in conversation. When someone has a problem, I find myself eager to help and often ready to blurt out an idea that would help before I have an agreement to work for the person. In these situations I now mentally check myself and, as tactfully as possible, say to the person that I have ideas about what he or she could do, but that since my revenue is generated from these ideas, I must reserve them. I then suggest that they can hire me and, for a fee, have the benefit of my ideas. To date, I have not found anyone who is offended by this explanation.

Freebies devalue your services

In fact, I think it makes them value my services even more. It certainly has made *me* value my services. Too many freebies can actually devalue your goods and services, not only in the mind of prospective clients but more frighteningly also in your own mind. If you devalue your goods and services in your own mind, how are you ever going to set profitable prices? If you can't justify to yourself what your goods and services are worth, how can you do so to someone else? Beware: Freebies must be used sparingly and wisely.

You see, giving away your goods or services to have a prospective client sample your business can be a valid marketing tool. Or, it can be unnecessary and a losing proposition. Before you give away your goods or services, ask yourself, "Is this necessary? Will I get business that I wouldn't have had by doing this? Am I getting some return on my investment of giving a freebie?"

Do not give a sampling of your services to a client with whom you have no track record and with whom you have no signed agreement to do business. While bonusing extra services to get a client's business may be a valid freebie, please refer to the upcoming chapter on pricing before doing so. Think through your freebies. Would you have had the business without giving them? How much did you spend, or expend, on prospective clients with freebies and still not get their business as a result?

Was your freebie profitable? If not, was it really worth your time and your profit to give that freebie?

Do charitable freebies get business?

Speaking of expending time on prospective clients brings me to the subject of charitable freebies. Too many small business people have a vague notion about charitable freebies. They think that charitable freebies will get them publicity and, hopefully, more business. In rare cases, this may be true. More often, these charitable freebies have no impact with direct business.

A few years into my business, I joined a local service organization. A client invited me to the initial meeting, at which I knew several people. One of these people, in encouraging me to join, stated that she got business after every meeting she attended. I initially was not interested in the organization as a way to get business, but rather as a way to give back to the community. However, I justified the $360 annual dues by saying to myself that I *may* generate business from my involvement.

So I joined the organization. In the four years of my involvement, I have received some business from its members, yes, but if I were to judge the success or failure of my involvement by the business it may have generated, I would be disappointed. Or, perhaps it is more accurate to say that *I* would be disappointing. I would be disappointing because there is more to life than always seeking business. Your involvement in organizations, whether service or otherwise, should be for reasons other than just to promote your business. There is a time for business and a time to give to yourself and a time to give back to your community. Yes, there will be overlap, and perhaps the friendships you make from your involvement will bring you business, and, if so, that's great! But don't join organizations with the sole purpose of generating business.

Your time is a freebie.

If you are really joining the organization, you are giving away another freebie. Whether you become involved on a basic level or a very active one, each organization that you join takes time. That time comes from somewhere. It either comes from your business or your personal time, and often, when you are a small business person, the boundary lines of personal and business time blur. As much as this sounds logical, it is easy to get pulled into organizations and then find that too much of your time is wrapped up in keeping the commitments they require.

I learned this the hard way.

When I started my business, I was heavily involved in the Western Wisconsin Ad Club. I had twice served as president for four year stints each and continued to head the Ad Day Committee and serve on the Awards Committee. These required a great deal of time. While yet a member of Ad Club, I joined the service organization. Then a group of business people from that service organization were interested in forming a Chippewa Valley women's business owners chapter of the Wisconsin Women Entrepreneurs. They invited me to the initial meeting, and since this was an organization that I felt would help me personally, I became quite involved. In fact, I was president for the first two plus years.

All three of these organizations took a great deal of my time. There were days, in fact, when all I did was work for these organizations. I had to prepare for a meeting. Or, I had to work on a project. Or, I had to communicate with other members of the organization. All this took time, and I was giving a great deal of freebie time. Was this too much?

Absolutely.

Freebie time steals from your business.

I realized that I could not give so much time to freebie organizations and grow my business, too. I knew that, in doing so, I was stealing from my business as well as robbing myself of personal time. Although I did not join these organizations to get business, I also could not justify the time commitment taken away from my business by saying that I got business from them.

What did I do about it? Well, time and circumstances helped me back off from these commitments. Ad Day died due to lack of attendance. Ad Club itself changed, and I dropped my membership. The women's group went through a metamorphosis, during which I left for almost a year, and although I am now back to attending meetings, I am no longer an officer. I still do belong to the service organization, and I am careful not to overextend myself in my involvement. Although I cannot say that I consciously took the bull by the horns and suddenly dropped out of these organizations, I did consciously recognize that I was expending too much time and energy in them. I needed to decrease that expenditure. As the circumstances warranted, I decreased my involvement and am now very vigilant as to how much I give.

As was always my focus, I am a part of these organizations not to develop business, but rather for personal development and community service. I recommend that you do the same. Give of your goods and services to charitable organizations. As you can afford it, give also of your time. Remember to do all this giving in the spirit of community betterment or for self growth. Do it consciously. Do not give with the expectation of getting business. Most likely, you will be disappointed if your efforts are strictly for obtaining business.

Be aware of your freebies.

Become acutely aware of freebies, both in time and services. Take time to stop and think the following about the freebie before you give it:

What do you expect this freebie to accomplish?

Is there a reasonable chance that you will achieve that result?

Do you have the time to deal with giving the freebie in either time, goods, or services?

Are you willing to accept the sacrifice that giving this freebie entails?

If you are willing to accept the sacrifice, and if you think giving the freebie will help your business or help yourself or help the community, give it. Just remember: Stop to think before you give freebies. Answer the above questions. Then make your decision about giving this freebie. Do your freebie-giving consciously with realistic expectations, and you will never regret giving a freebie.

5
The Power of No

Let's face it, for most of us, *no* is a difficult word to say, especially to clients. Sometime during my first five years in business, I read that if you are doing business with all prospective clients with whom you come in contact, you are doing something wrong. The day I fully accepted that statement is the day my business began to make a profit.

It was the day I learned to say *no* to clients.

This *no* may be in the form of not working with a client from the onset. Or, the *no* may involve being realistic about your time and letting a client know that you don't have the time right now to work on the client's project. Or, the *no* may be dropping unprofitable clients and not doing business with them in the future. All of these are difficult to do because each client seems to equal revenue, and why would you ever say *no* to revenue?

Is your client a revenue or an expense?

While some clients appear to be revenue, they are, in actuality, an expense.

How can a client be an expense when clients pay you revenue? Have you ever, with any client, and at any time, either before, during, or after, your dealings with a client, evaluated how much the client cost you?

I finally did.

Granted, there are always hard costs, such as office supplies and materials, in dealing with clients. But where a client really costs a business money is the time a business spends with a client, not only time spent face-to-face and in meetings with a client, but also time spent thinking about a client, working on a client's project, and the insidious time spent emotionally tied-up reacting to a client's actions.

Let's look at a very basic example of this that every business encounters, i.e., a client who does not pay the invoice on time. Beyond the time spent contacting the client to pay, how much emotional and, consequently, energy drain does this situation take from whoever is making the contact and, perhaps, others in your business? How much time is spent venting frustrations about a client who has not paid? How much more could be accomplished if the time spent venting these frustrations was used toward developing more business?

If you could, or would, tally up this time, you would be amazed.

Now, consider difficult clients. One client is never satisfied the first time and makes you virtually start from scratch more than once. Another difficult client just crawls under your skin and irritates you every time you do business with him or her. Again, beyond the time spent with the client, how much does the irritation of dealing with these clients bleed over into your work with other clients? How much is your efficiency affected? How much of your personal time is drained because you think about or talk about this irritating client?

I bet it's more than you think.

Why we deal with irritating clients

Why do we do business with clients like this? It's simple; we want the money, and these clients can give it to us. It doesn't matter how many hoops we must jump through. It doesn't matter that we live in irritation. It doesn't matter that they take more of our time. We want the money, and they can give it to us.

For this very reason, I did business with one client who was a time-drainer. She always liked my ideas, and I liked her as a person. But every time we got into a project together, she was never satisfied with the first creation. She often didn't like the first nor the second, and she thought the third was mediocre. It's understandable that a client may not like the first creation or may want to make minor changes. But with her it was a pattern. She didn't really know what she wanted and micromanaged each project to the point of her having difficulty ever getting the project completed. Then, just when I thought everything was fine, she started picking apart sections of the project she had previously approved. Unfortunately for her, she ran her business the same way and encountered many challenges doing so.

I spent more hours than I had anticipated on her projects and did not get paid for these hours. I started on retainer with her, and once I got off that unprofitable system, did work with her on a project basis. When I quoted the project, I padded extra hours in anticipation of her micromanaging, but even that could not cover the frustration of my never being able to satisfy her. In addition, the last time I worked with her, not only was she slow in paying her bill, but she attempted not to pay me. Without my knowledge, she queried vendors who were involved in the projects for which she owed me about a couple of problems. She questioned the vendors as to whether these problems were my responsibility or theirs. Luckily, the vendors were honest and verified that the responsibility was theirs, not mine.

I knew from having worked with her that she had disputed work with other vendors and, subsequently, had not paid them, and I knew it was only a matter of time before I was subjected to the same treatment. Topping off all the "extra," unpaid time I had given her, not to mention the hours of irritation in doing business with her, with the possibility of not getting paid at all, sent me into the *no* zone.

Saying no can be painful.

I have a problem saying *no*. It is against my nature. In fact, it is almost painful for me to say *no*, especially when it comes to making money. But I broke through to saying my first *no* to this client because of this low pay, possibly *no* pay, situation. I evaluated how much time and energy working with her drained from my business and realized that I could make more money and have a more enjoyable life not working with her. I resolved not to do business with her again. I realized the power of *no*.

No has a freedom inside it. *No* gives you control over your time and your energy. Using it at the right time, before you get into unprofitable dealings with a client, exercises its power to make you money.

After this experience, I resolved to say *no* more quickly, preferably before working with a client, or in the early stages of working with a client if I detected problems. The first client I said *no* to working with at all was an artist who had wonderful potential but could make more money more quickly by marketing his work. Our initial meeting was cordial, and I broke my freebie rule by throwing out lots of ideas, all of which he liked. We left the date of our second meeting open, and I promised to get back to him within the week to set its date. Before I could call him, he called me, several times in fact. I was in the throes of finishing a large project and was wrapped up in it. He called me relentlessly on my cell phone demanding an appointment. You may think he sounded eager to go forward with his marketing, which was true, but there was a tone in his voice and an unsettling pattern in his calls that triggered my "red alert, problem client" gut feelings.

I scheduled the appointment with him and told him at that appointment that we would not work well together. I said *no*. Was it hard! I had trouble telling him why I was saying *no*. First of all, it's difficult to explain a gut feeling acquired from the experiences of working with others who were difficult. Then, I was applying these experience lessons to him as a new client. He was not happy, to say the least. Secondarily, as I said before, it's very painful for me to say no. My stomach was tied in a churning knot for hours afterward, and I felt guilty for days.

Through it all, however, I felt certain that I had done the right thing.

More recently, an organization requested that I conceptualize and sell sponsorships for a show. After an initial meeting with the person running the organization, I agreed to sell the sponsorships. At the time I thought, or perhaps assumed, that I would be dealing only with the head person and that he would make all the decisions. In retrospect I should have been alerted to a potential problem regarding decision-making. While he initiated the original contact, each meeting thereafter was attended not only by him but also several other people, all of whom proceeded to get involved in the decision-making. About six weeks into this project, I realized that I was breaking my rules by dealing with a committee. The committee was changing the ground rules we had originally set down, and each member was wanting to be kept informed of all my actions. When I was negotiating a deal with a sponsor, all the committee members wanted input. While one might agree to the terms, another would have a different view, making it very difficult to finalize terms with a potential sponsor. The money that

I made was based on commissions from sold sponsorships. Because of the committee's actions, these were looking much more difficult to sell than I had originally anticipated. Increasingly, I felt that the possibility of selling sponsorships was slim. It seemed likely that I would make nothing. I realized that I was putting in time with a low likelihood of return.

The freedom of no

I gathered my courage, met with the committee, and told them I was ending my work on the project. Was this easy to do? No. I found it difficult to explain, but I told the truth. I told them that I didn't work with committees and that I hadn't realized this would be a committee situation when I was initially approached on the project. I recommended that since they had a sense of what they wanted done, they were wisest to implement their program themselves. The freedom I felt after that meeting was energizing! By saying *no*, I gained a great deal of time and energy to apply toward profitable work instead of putting time into a project with increasingly little hope of return.

To add profit to your bottom line, learn to say *no*. It's hard to say *no*. That's why so many people say, *maybe* when they really mean *no*. Exercise your courage, and learn to say *no*. You'll find a freedom and a power that you didn't expect. You'll also find more profit because *no* enables you to keep focused on *your* goals, not someone else's.

6
Pricing: You Can Always Go Down, But You Can't Go Up

How much is too much, and how little is too little? Most of us charge too little. Why? We live with a fear that we will not get the business. What happens if that fear is realized and we don't get the business? Try following your fear of not getting business. Ask yourself, "What's the worst that would happen if I don't get this business?" Your answer will somehow involve the suffering of your business's bottom line. Who suffers if your business's bottom line suffers? Perhaps your employees, but ultimately you, right? In fact, you stand to suffer the most. You are the ultimate sufferer from not getting business. That is why we all live in fear of turning away business because of price. That is why we often charge too little.

Under-payment burns you out.

But what is the result of time after time getting underpaid for your efforts? Although you may stay in business, you exist at a level substandard to what you could be existing, and eventually this level wears you down and burns you out. This is a principal reason why 60% of small businesses fail in the first ten years. The owners get tired. They get tired of putting out so much for so little. They get tired of settling for less than their expertise is worth. The reasons they went into business blur, and their efforts make them feel like a rat on one of those spinning wheel toys.

Unfortunately, they stuck themselves in that rat cage and climbed on that spinning toy all by themselves. I've noticed as a marketing consultant that every time a client wants to stimulate business, his or her first reaction is to offer a discount, have a sale, or reduce the price in some way. I have not yet seen a survey that shows the number one reason customers do business with a company is the price. Generally, price is fourth on the list. So why is a business so eager to drop its prices?

They don't thoroughly think the price through before they slap it onto the product or service.

What goes into pricing?

Let's start from the point of view of the business. First, and quite obviously, hard costs of the product or materials provided in the service need to be considered. These costs include the freight, taxes, transportation, and other additional out-of-pocket costs in getting the product or materials to the customer. Next the labor, whether it is that of an employee or the business owner, is added to the fee. Traditionally, overhead is factored in, and a profit is added to the top. This is how most businesses arrive at their prices.

But they've missed a very important consideration. What is that product or service worth to the potential buyer?

Pricing from the customer's point-of-view

Let's take price from the point of view of the customer. The customer cares about only one thing: what's in it for me? What does this product or service do for me? Does it make my life easier? Does it save me money? Does it give me better use of my time? Does it bring me more income? What is the end result for the customer of having done business with your business?

Think this through. If you can't clearly answer these questions, call up five of your good customers and ask them. Tell them you appreciate their business, and to serve other customers well, you want to know what they like about doing business with your company. What do you think they will say? How do you think they will feel?

They will be flattered that you asked their opinions, and they will tell you exactly why they do business with you. And, the interest you showed in them by seeking their opinions will solidify your business relationship with them even more strongly.

More importantly, you will be able to answer the question: What is the end result of your customers' having done business with your business? With that information, you can now look at your pricing from the customers' point of view.

What *is* that point of view? Does your product or service make life easier, save money or time, or bring in more money? Does your customer appreciate your promptness, reliability, or dependability?

Price is not the first consideration

Construction and home improvement businesses are notorious for being slow to respond to requests for bids, slow to get projects moving, and often behind in completing projects. I was teaching a marketing session in an entrepreneurship class recently when a participant who works in the construction industry adamantly challenged my contention that price is not the number one factor in a customer's decision. "In construction," he said, "the lowest bid always gets the job." I asked him if he would take the lowest bid from *any* subcontractor. More specifically, would he even consider a bid from a subcontractor who had a reputation for poor quality workmanship? "No," he replied. "I wouldn't." So price *wasn't his* first consideration.

Nor is price the first consideration of homeowners. What do homeowners want? They want the job done right the first time. They want prompt attention to their job. They want communication during the entire process of the job as to its progress. They want the mess cleaned up after the job is completed. And, of course, they want a fair price. Most homeowners would tell you that they would pay more for a company who completes the job correctly, is prompt, communicates with them regularly, and cleans up after itself.

What are homeowners buying?

They are buying a home, a place where they feel comfortable and a place of which they are proud. They are not buying a price.

When you hire bookkeepers or accountants, is price your first consideration? No. Your first consideration is can they do the job. Can they help you save money? Can they help you fulfill your reporting obligations to the government? Do they have the knowledge and experience that you want? Will they give you good service and follow-through?

How much is it worth to you that they have knowledge and experience? How much is it worth to you that they do the job correctly? How much is it worth to you that you have fulfilled your legal obligations to the government?

Perhaps a great deal.

If you consider the consequences of bookkeepers or accountants who do not know what they are doing, a larger fee may be insignificant. What's it worth to you to avoid trouble with the IRS? What's it worth to you that all revenues and expenses are recorded accurately? What's it worth to you to have a clear picture of your cash flow? It's worth a great deal.

You may now be saying, "These are service industry examples. It's easy to differentiate and price service industries, but products are price sensitive." Yes, products are more easily compared than service industries because of products' uniformity. But beyond the product itself is the experience customers have in obtaining the product. Is it easy to deal with the company selling the product? Are staff polite? Is service prompt? What is the return policy? How much does the company really care that the customer is satisfied? Would you pay a higher price for a product from a company that is easy to deal with and will make sure you are happy with your purchase?

Over time you will. After the first time you buy an item from someone who treats you poorly when problems arise, thereafter you will consider the company's reputation when making a purchase. Why? Because you realize that what you are truly buying is what you want that product or service to do for you. You are not buying the price.

Pricing was a mystery.

When I started my business, pricing was a mystery to me. I had no idea where to start. I knew where I didn't want to be. I didn't want to be paid hourly because that has the potential to create questions in clients' minds. Clients may wonder, "How much time did this take? Are these full hours, or do parts of an hour count as a full hour?" Questions such as these about hourly pay can lead to distrust between you and your clients. In addition, hourly work is a time drain to track. When you're a one person show, as I am, that time drain makes a difference. Plus, I didn't want to do it!

Another way for me to price my business was on a percentage basis, traditional advertising agency pricing. The agency gets paid a percentage of all monies booked with media, usually 15-20%. This pricing did not work for me since I was a marketing consultant and not an advertising agency. I also didn't want to be paid on a percentage basis because I am not a believer in rewarding people to spend my money, which is what percentage basis pricing appears to do.

From my direct questioning of potential clients before I started my business, I knew that businesses wanted to know their costs up front. They didn't want surprises later. Therefore, I determined to give them quotes up front of how much a project would cost and not exceed that quote. My first five years I always billed as quoted...or less. Yes, there were times, in fact, when I did bill less than quoted because the project did not take the time that I had anticipated.

How did I decide what to quote?

I computed the amount of time that I projected the job would take times the amount that I wanted to make per hour. Since I was in a steep learning curve the first months and years of my business, I often took more time to do the job than I had anticipated. I never told the client of the additional time that I had expended on a project nor did I ask for additional pay. I always stuck with my quote and absorbed the difference because I felt that it would be wrong to make the customer pay for my learning.

Looking back, this was a mistake.

Perhaps ethically, it was fair not to pass on the entire price to customers, but for the health of my business, and my own personal health, it was close to being disastrous. The extra stress and worry that I created for myself from not being paid for the entire time I spent on a project almost burned me out. Then add to that the loss of income from projects that I did not do because I didn't have the time. Added together, the combination of stress and lack of time wore me down and stymied my business. I can't begin to calculate how much more business I might have had but didn't pursue due to lack of time.

And that wasn't the only way I underpriced myself.

Often, I would compute the price of the project and then look at the business and think, "They will not pay this much." Consequently, I would lower my price.

Talk about shooting myself in the foot! Talk about not considering pricing from the buyer's point of view! Talk about putting myself and my business on the fast track to burnout!

I was there.

Pricing was uncomfortable

The first months and years of my business I felt uncomfortable with the whole concept of pricing my services. I was uncomfortable with setting the price. I was uncomfortable with presenting the price to the customer. I was uncomfortable with invoicing the job.

Interestingly, throughout those months and years, I never had any price resistance from my customers.

That tells you something, doesn't it?

Yes, I'm sure they would have paid more.

How did I learn that I was making a mistake and change my pricing?

As I grew in confidence regarding my knowledge and expertise, I also noticed that many businesses that were failing often had the same complaints. "We don't get enough business. We're tired. Customers are cheap." I became more and more intrigued by pricing. As I mentioned before, I noted that every business owner always addressed price first when it came to stimulating business. Was there a connection?

Yes. All of us were not considering pricing from the customer's point of view.

What would the customer pay for a business's

products or services? No one knew because no one, including me, had ever asked.

How much will a customer pay?

Upon reflection, I realized that my customer valued my services more than I did. My customer would pay more for my services than what I was asking. My customer thought he or she was getting a great deal. It was a better deal than I had intended to give them.

The problem with my pricing did not stem from my customer. The problem came directly from me. The problem resided in my head and my heart.

Once I made this realization, what did I do?

I started by raising my value first in my mind and then in the fee that I asked the customer for my services. I increased my prices gradually, in baby steps. Once in a while, I met price resistance, and consequently a business did not do business with me. You know what? That was wonderful! Please don't think that I was masochistic or that I wanted to turn away customers. However, to avoid burnout, I realized that I would not be able to work with everyone. The limited number of hours in a day and the limited amount of energy that I had available restricted me. In turn, I needed to restrict my number of clients.

You can't do business with everyone.

I learned that I couldn't do business with everyone.

I learned not to work with "unprofitable" clients. Who are "unprofitable" clients? They are people who have the least amount to pay you but want you to do the most for that money. They want to be certain that they "get their money's worth."

This is particularly a problem with retainers. When you are working for a specified amount of money for a specified period of time without specifying the amount of work that is included, you are setting yourself up on a retainer basis that is guaranteed to be unprofitable. I know. I set myself up on retainer that way. In retrospect it seems really stupid to me, but I established the retainer at the time to have a steady income. Knowing that I had a certain amount of money coming in each month gave me security and comfort. I could count on that money. Of course, this retainer money could disappear just as quickly as any other money, but I didn't view it that way. The retainer money was money that I didn't need to find. It was already there, or so it seemed.

In reality, the retainer money limited my business because I spent more time with the retainer clients, so that they "got their money's worth," than I had anticipated when I established the retainer agreement. This lowered my hourly fee. By giving extra "unpaid" hours to the retainer client, I was kept from seeking additional clients. Too much of my time was tied up in the retainer client to do so. As a result, the price of my time and services was lowered, not just for the retainer client, but for my overall business as well. I was making my business affordable to anyone who wanted my services in order to have money coming in.

Under-pricing leads to an unprofitable business.

I came to the realization that if I underprice my services so that I am affordable to all, I will burn myself out and have an unprofitable business. Even though price isn't the first consideration in a buying decision, clients' budgets do, or should, have limits. These limits may be a constraint to using all of my services. If that is the case, I can either *not* do business with those customers or perform fewer services for them. Conforming my pricing to what their budgets could handle and, in the bargain, including *all* my services was only hurting me and my business.

I began to realize that customers were willing to pay more for my services. Looking at it from their point of view, I realized that what I did for them saved them frustration, time, and money---plus, more importantly, made them profit. What was that worth to them? More than I was charging.

Under-pricing hurts your customer, too.

If you underprice your business so that your business and you suffer, the customer is the loser too.

How?

Your underpricing will lead to an inability to serve your customer well. Underpricing will weaken you and your business because you will not get the income you want and your business will not have the cash flow it requires. In a worst case, underpricing could weaken your business enough to lead to its demise. A weakened or out-of-business company helps no one, neither you nor your customer. If your customer no longer has access to your services, for whatever the reason, how has your underpriced service served your customer?

It hasn't.

If your business is unavailable to perform a service, your customer must find a new company to do that service. Then, your customer must train that new company in the manner in which your customer wants the service done. Your customer loses both time and money in doing so. It is much easier and more profitable for your customer to pay you more for your services and keep doing business with your company than to underpay you and find a replacement when your company's services are no longer available.

Do both your business and your customer's business a favor. Learn from my mistake in pricing. Price your business's products and services from the customer's point of view to insure the health of your business. Do your research on what that customer's point of view is before setting your prices, and set them right the first time. If a customer's budget constraints won't allow you to do all you'd like, do less and do it well.

Remember, in setting your prices, you can always go down by doing less, but you can't go up. You must justify a higher price to your customer. Your customer will not pay you more merely because you want more pay. Hence, establish prices from the start that make your bottom line profitable. Do not burn yourself out by underpricing your products or services. Both you *and your customer* will be glad you established prices from the start which will ensure your business's profitability.

7
Contracts: Never Start Work without One.

When I started my business, I thought a person's word was a solid basis on which to do business. I thought asking clients to sign an agreement would be an affront. In my mind, this request appeared to question their honesty. Several experiences taught me otherwise.

Agreements clarify work.

I learned that while a client may verbally agree to do business with me, unless I have an agreement, the terms of that relationship are murky and can lead to problems. By terms I am referring to payment, termination, and all those traditional legal specifics which are important. I am also referring to the particulars: what your work entails, what you will and will not do, and what you do and do not promise. These work particulars are extremely important to your business's profitability because if you don't outline them clearly, you may find yourself doing work that you had not intended to do and, consequently, not getting paid for it. You may also find yourself responsible for promises you had not made or, more specifically, promises that were inferred because you had not clearly stated that they were not made.

One experience I had in this regard involved one of my first clients. This was during my pre-written agreement days. We verbally agreed, in general terms, that I would handle the client's marketing, which meant *whatever* the client designated as marketing. The client would pay me a specified monthly retainer for those services. I found myself doing a great deal more work than I originally had intended and, consequently, making much less per hour than I had projected. At times this client was difficult to reach because he was so busy. Hence, I spent additional time chasing him down for consultations and approvals.

Did I discuss this with the client? No. I was too insecure in my business to bring up the subject. I feared in doing so that I risked losing the client. Beyond that insecurity, though, I also had nothing on paper to define the parameters of my work. So I really had nothing to complain about. By not having a written agreement, I had limited my options and shot myself in the foot. The lack of a written agreement inadvertently placed me in an uncomfortable position wherein the client held all the power rather than having the client and myself on an equal footing. Inequality between you and a client leads to loss of control for you and loss of your services's value for the client.

Written agreements are professional.

Think about it. Who do you respect more, someone with whom you have a written agreement, or someone with whom you have a verbal approval? Who is more professional in your mind? Who is more valued? With whom are you more likely to adhere to the conditions of your agreement because you can refer to those conditions in writing?

Written agreements clarify the terms of the relationship, which is a benefit to both parties.

Consider what happened to me with a client who wanted to change the terms of our written agreement. Instead of paying me the agreed upon fee, he wanted to change to a commission payment and, in the bargain, wanted to change my responsibilities from marketing to include management. I did not want to do this and told him so. I wanted out and subsequently terminated the relationship, sending him an invoice for my services and reimbursements for paid outs. He delayed and delayed and delayed payment. Finally I took him to court, which I felt comfortable doing because I had a written agreement. Unfortunately, I had to settle for less than the full amount because he was from another state and promised to stall payment forever across state lines unless I did so. However, I was pleased that I had given myself a solid footing in court and more leverage with him because of my written agreement. As a result, I did get *some* revenue, rather than no revenue, from the client.

Written agreements protect you.

Written agreements are a protection for you in so many ways. They spell out the parameters of the work to be done, how it will be done, and when it will be done. They also help you get paid. They are invaluable in protecting you from a client's projection of unstated expectations or a client's declaration of what they *think* you promised.

Speaking of expectations, I will tell you about a situation which had disaster written all over it from the start. Through the request of a good, long-standing client of mine, I met with an association, gave them some ideas, and agreed to do specific work for them in a short period of time. I say it had disaster written all over it because it violated several of my cardinal rules: don't work with a committee, don't do work because a friend asks you to, and don't work too close to the vest. Nonetheless, I ignored my rules and my gut feeling in an attempt to "help" my client and his association.

Fortunately, I clearly wrote in the agreement what I would do and did not promise an outcome. I say *fortunately* because I ended up doing several things not stated in my agreement, and the association ended up expecting an outcome that they had in their minds but had not communicated to me. More specifically, the outcome was in the mind of a person involved with the association. In that person's mind, the outcome was not achieved. Consequently, they sent me a check for a reduced amount, half of the agreed upon fee, along with a note stating that since the outcome had not been what they had expected, they considered paying me nothing but decided to graciously send me half of the fee. Although I felt badly that their outcome had not been achieved, I also realized that in my business I can do certain things but can never promise what the results will be. There are just too many uncontrollable factors in marketing to be able to promise results.

Because I had a written agreement which clearly stated what I would do and did not promise outcomes, I replied to their letter with a letter of my own. My letter stated the agreed upon fee, the fact that I had done the work stated, and that we had not negotiated a reduction of my fee. Furthermore, I wrote that if I did not receive the check for the full amount by a certain date, I would take them to court. The date the check was due I received a call from the association's office saying it was being sent that day, and I did, indeed, receive the check for the full amount the next day. Without the written agreement, I would have had nothing to back up what we had agreed upon and would have lost half, if not all, of the fee for my work.

Agreements protect you, and they protect the client. A written agreement is a clear communication of what your relationship with your client entails. It also either states outrightly or implies what the relationship does *not* entail.

Do not leave inferences.

As much as possible, agreements should state exactly and clearly what the agreement entails and not leave anything to be inferred. This doesn't mean your agreement must be a huge document. Mine are usually one page. In my agreements, I state exactly what activities I will perform. I specify a time period of the agreement. I detail how much I will be paid and when that payment will occur. I highlight that this payment is for my services only and does not include the services or fees of other vendors or organizations. I note items such as postage or paper, for which I will be reimbursed.

Include termination clause.

I also include a termination clause. You may be thinking, "Why would you want to talk termination?" First, anyone who is professional and will follow-through on performing the work has no difficulty discussing a termination arrangement at the onset of the relationship. If you are unsettled about doing so, ask yourself why? Are you insecure about losing the job? Are you worried about completing what you are promising to do? Are you concerned that the client may exercise the termination clause? If you have that much unease about the client, reexamine if you want to do business with him or her. If you have said you will do something that you are not certain you can complete or complete in a satisfactory manner, express this to the client before you sign an agreement that states you will do so. If you are insecure about losing the job, have a talk with yourself about the origin of your insecurity. Where is your insecurity coming from, and what can you do about it?

I've given you an example of an agreement for a service business, but these ideas also are applicable to retail and manufacturer's businesses. Retailers can apply these ideas to both service industry firms with whom they do business and to vendors with whom they write purchase orders. Always have a paper trail of what you ordered, including shipment dates, payment dates, terms, return policy, and other specifics that clearly define your receipt of the goods and outline your responsibilities regarding the goods. If you order verbally and do not keep a record of that order and do not have the terms of the order on paper, you have no recourse to anything that happens with that order or to anything that happens to your business because of it. Written orders and terms are a protection for both the retailer and the manufacturer. And that's why manufacturers also need clearly written order terms and clearly written agreements with their vendors.

What's in your written agreements?

Do you have one for every client? If not, create a written agreement for each one of your clients and have it signed by both the client and you. Give your client a copy with both signatures, too. Do you put your orders and agreements with vendors in writing? If not, do so today. Have your vendors sign the agreement and, again, give them a copy with both signatures. Contracts or written agreements: Never start work or do business without them.

8

Billing: Get a Grip on It.

Billing is a necessary but pesky subject. It sounds like a simple subject, doesn't it? In theory, yes, but in practice, it is not.

Why?

When you are starting your business, your focus is first on getting work and then on getting the work completed well and in a timely manner. Your focus is not on billing. I know this sounds stupid because if your focus is not on billing, how are you ever getting paid? Well, you tend not to get paid in a very steady manner because you do not bill in a very steady manner.

How can you be so unprepared for billing?

Before I started my business, I read that the number one downfall of small businesses was billing. This seemed incomprehensible to me. How could billing be that difficult, I thought? I discovered how.

System of billing

First, you need a system of billing, which wisely would be established before you start your business. I didn't do that in the beginning, and I suspect many others have not done that either. It's difficult to conceive of billing when you are wondering if you will even get work. When you get your first work, you eagerly complete it, and then you excitedly move on to the next job.

Just as I was, you are likely unprepared with an

invoice, an invoicing system, and a recordkeeping system. To generate an invoice, you need to set one up in your computer or print forms for your use. Many software programs that are standard on computers today offer invoice forms. You can quickly adapt one for your business. You need to set up an invoicing system so that you can track if an invoice was paid, when it was paid, and how it was paid. Further, you need to record these payments in a recordkeeping system that not only tells you about your payments but also gives you a financial picture of your business. This financial picture is important for you to review on a regular basis and for you to present to financial institutions if you are interested in borrowing money.

When do you do your billing?

Second, you need a plan of when the billing is to be handled. I tried different plans. I tried billing monthly, but then the end of the month would come and go, and suddenly, it would be the middle of the next month. I would not yet have finished my billing from the previous month. Sometimes this happened for two or three months in a row. I also tried billing weekly, which worked no better than monthly.

As I was finishing this book, a graphic artist friend of mine who has her own business told me that she recently changed her billing to weekly. Rather than waiting for a project to be completed, she is billing the client for the hours that she worked on a project at the end of each week. She is now billing 52 times a year. After a month or two, she has found this system to work extremely well. Her cash flow has increased tremendously, and her clients appreciate the opportunity to spread their payments over weeks, rather than pay in one lump sum. Weekly billing also communicates to her clients how much time she has put into a project. Therefore, her communication with her clients has also improved. Her clients know by the weekly billing that their project is getting her attention and just how much attention the project is receiving.

She has taken years, just as I have, to discover a billing time table that is fair to herself, her business's cashflow, and her clients. She, too, has tried different methods, which is very typical for entrepreneurs. We learn by trial and error what method works best for us. How could I financially survive this while I tested these billing time frames? It was a financial roller coaster ride. Eventually, the backup account from which I was surviving would get low, and then I would give attention to billing because it had become a high priority. Unfortunately, at that point, I often had to wait 30 days or more to get the payments. This, of course, was all due to my inattention to billing.

Finally, I started billing upon completion of the project. Once I schooled myself not only to start but also to maintain this practice, I have conquered my billing problem. For me, this process makes the most sense because, in general, I do not have a business that does monthly work. I do have a couple of clients who are on a monthly billing, and I can still find myself falling behind in getting their billing out. But most of my work is on a project basis. As a wrap-up to the project, I bill the client.

This system has helped my cash flow enormously and eased tensions between my clients and me about billing. Initially, I had clients who sometimes hadn't received their billing for months. While many clients were happy to delay payment, some became testy that they had not been billed promptly. As I sit here writing this, that seems quite embarrassing to me. At the time, I was not avoiding billing intentionally. (Really, billing is not difficult.)

Billing is not my usual activity.

Principally, I did not attend to my billing because I was focused on working for my clients, and billing was not an activity that was directly working for my clients. Billing was an activity that was working for me and my business. In addition, billing was such a different activity from my work. Marketing was creative, while billing was rote work. It was no fun! I enjoyed working for my clients, but I didn't enjoy billing.

You see, my work involves thinking, creativity, and ideas. Billing involves forms, numbers, and processes. The two are very different. To switch from one to the other requires a switch in using another side of my brain, obviously one that does not like being exercised very often.

Billing seems anticlimactic to me because, after all, the project is completed and the money has been earned. It seems like such a nuisance to fill out that piece of paper to get paid. Can't the client just pay me?

Yes, yes, I do understand accounting and billing. What I just said is my dominant brain or my laziness talking. This leads me to the third suggestion on billing. Delegate it, or hire it handled. I have not yet done this. Why? I work on a system in which I quote each client the price of the job prior to my starting work. Sometimes in the course of getting the job completed, I pay out monies that need to be reimbursed. By the time I collect the paid outs along with the quotes and then hand them over to someone else to do the billing, I could have generated the invoices myself. So time-wise, it seems that I will accomplish little to nothing in having someone else handle my billing.

However, as I write this, I see that a bookkeeper could help me a great deal. I may not have a bookkeeper do my billing initially because it is still easier and quicker to generate my own invoices, but a bookkeeper could take the rest of the financial recordkeeping off my back. A bookkeeper could insure that the recordkeeping was entered monthly and on time. This regular recordkeeping would help me keep better track of my business's numbers and, consequently, enable me to see where my business is headed. And getting familiar and comfortable with a bookkeeper might encourage me eventually, perhaps quite quickly, to turn over the invoicing too. Stay tuned, maybe not having used a bookkeeper/accountant will be a mistake that I correct my second five years in business.

Underneath my explanations for my billing problems lie a couple of other reasons why I handle my own billing. One, I do not want to pay out the money to have my billing handled by someone else if I can avoid it, and two, I am accustomed to working alone, doing my own thing. Call me cheap, and call me a lone wolf. Both are part of who I am. I have recently been reading a series of books by Robert Kiyosaki, the Rich Dad Poor Dad series. Robert emphasizes hiring a team of professionals including bookkeepers or accountants to help you with your business. He points out that the money is well spent to get the expertise and the objective viewpoint of these professionals. I can see his point.

Eliminate the stress of billing.

In addition to the expertise and objectivity that professionals offer, they also make you look good. I have had many stressful moments over billing late, not staying on top of accounts, and forgetting to bill for reimbursements or additional work. I can eliminate this stress by having a professional handle my invoicing and recordkeeping. We all want to reduce our stress whenever possible, don't we?

You also will help your reputation by using a professional. When I look back over my billing delays, I realize that untimely billing did not help my reputation and status with my clients. How foolish is it to work hard and do a good job for a client and then irritate your client with delayed billing? To my knowledge, I did not lose future work over the irritation, but since a reputation takes so much to earn, why deliberately mess with it yourself? Why not insure that you will continue to look good by having a professional handle your billing?

If I had had a professional handling my invoicing, I also may have collected some accounts that were uncollectible. Overall, I have had few uncollectible accounts. In my first five years of business, I only had one account from which I received no payment, and an additional three who did not pay me the full amount. Had I kept abreast of those accounts with whom I had problems, I probably would have collected more. Or I may have stopped working with them sooner, which would have freed my time to work with a paying client. Either way, my business, my cash flow, and my income would have improved.

Be good to yourself, your business, and your cash flow. If you are thinking of starting a business, set up your invoicing and recordkeeping system before you start, even if you have nothing to record. If you are already in business, review your invoicing and recordkeeping system. Do you have one? Is it handled by a professional? If not, why not? Do you have a plan as to when you invoice? Who does your invoicing? Can you improve your invoicing and recordkeeping? If so, do it!

Learn from my mistakes. Develop a healthier business by getting a grip on your billing. You'll reduce stress on yourself and have a more profitable business.

9
Desperation Can Be a Paralyzing, Limiting Feeling.

Have you ever felt desperate?

Desperation is born from fear. (Fear of not enough business. Fear of not enough money. Fear of failure.) This fear ties you in a knot and paralyzes you from addressing just what will help you the most. Fear creates inaction.

Inaction is like a snowball that is rolling downhill but gets stopped at a rock. The rock holds it in place, and eventually the inaction of just sitting there leaves the snowball subject to the effects of the elements, such as melting from the sun. When the snowball was rolling downhill picking up momentum and more snow as it rolled, the elements had little to no effect on it. But without the addition of fresh snow and the movement of rolling downhill, the snowball gets smaller and smaller.

Likewise, you and your business get smaller and smaller when you let the fear of desperation tie you into inaction.

What leads you to feel desperate?

For me, it was losing a client, which meant losing business and, ultimately, revenue.

Losing a client leads to desperation.

When I had a sense that I might be losing a client, or that things were not quite right with a client, I went into avoidance mode with that client. I put off calling the client. I procrastinated on his or her work. Even the thought of seeing the client made my stomach churn.

One client that I avoided had a small shop for which I'd developed a marketing plan. Part of the agreement was to implement the plan. The first implementation was a series of direct mail pieces which we planned to drop in consecutive months starting in February and going through June. Due to a family illness, I didn't get the pieces created until February, and then one delay after another followed. The owner went on a winter vacation. The shop's principal employee had to be replaced. Memorial Day, a holiday, was not a good time to mail the piece. Eventually, rather than a February through June monthly mailing, the mailer was sent monthly from July through November.

By this time I was feeling increasingly worried about the results of the mailers. Would they bring in the business that the shop needed? Was our timing correct? What would happen to the shop if it didn't get the business? This worry not only increased, but it kept me from seeing the client and asking how the mailing was working. For months this worry and inaction accumulated into a desperate feeling.

Why? Because of fear.

The fear of losing a client made me feel desperate, and when I felt desperate I became inactive toward that client.

Not only was I inactive in seeing the client, I also was inactive in billing him over several months as the agreement stated. I was inactive in implementing the rest of the plan, partly from his suggestion to wait. Whatever the reasons, my activity with the client came to a halt and led to an increasingly strong feeling of desperation that I was going to lose the account.

Now, logically, you're thinking, "Well, of course, if you are inactive, you are going to lose the client. Duh!" You're right, and I knew that, too. But when you're feeling worried, then guilty, and then desperate, no amount of logic can reason with those emotions.

It is difficult to reason with fear. In order to grow your business, facing your fear is your only option.

Fear leads to inaction.

Until you face that fear, you affect your entire business. You see, unfortunately, my inaction in this situation bled over into the rest of my business too. I found myself thinking about this situation throughout the day. It resided as "mental garbage" in my head. It slowed down my work. It left me with a continuous vague feeling of something unfinished. I could not rid myself of it. Not only did I have a more difficult time getting through the day, but my output suffered also. It reminded me of another situation in which my fear had led me to inaction.

I had a service industry client with whom I had been doing business for several years. This client's daughter was pursuing a graphic arts degree and becoming increasingly involved in the business. For months, I could feel the handwriting on the wall. She would want to take over the marketing. And, if you were in her parents' place, why wouldn't you give her the experience and save money in the bargain?

I slowed down my calls to this client. Once our fall project was completed, nothing was in the works, which made it easier to delay seeing them. I was on a monthly retainer with this business, and I dreaded losing that regular source of income. For several weeks I agonized over the pending loss of this account. The income from this client was not large, but it *was* constant. Having the security of a constant stream of income, whatever its size, was comfortable. With it, I could face each month knowing that I had some revenue coming in that month. As the weeks passed, my anxiety grew until it reached a point at which the worry outweighed the potential loss of income. I wanted to get this situation resolved.

Finally, in December, I gathered my courage and made an appointment to meet with the client. Just as predicted, the client told me that my services were no longer needed because their daughter would be handling their marketing in the future. It was a friendly parting with much appreciation on the owners' part for my assistance, but the bottom line for me was the loss of a client and, consequently, the loss of income.

Through my fear of loss, I forced myself to look for the positives in the situation. Even though the retainer had been nice, the hourly fee was low because I had spent more hours on the account than I had originally intended. Hence, not having the account enabled me to do business with another account, or two, or even three for the same amount of time and make more money. Yes, at the time I did wonder where I would find those accounts. In teaching myself how to handle desperation, I resolved not to worry about where accounts would come from, but rather to keep working at getting accounts and trust that they *would* come.

I also stopped doing business on retainer. (But that's another chapter.)

Desperation limits your business.

Upon reflection, I learned that my feeling of desperation born from my fear of loss of income had done more than emotionally tie me up in knots. Desperation had limited my business. Spending time feeling desperate had sapped time and energy that I could have used working with other clients, searching for new clients, or enjoying personal time. My desperation had hurt me in more ways than one.

I resolved not to let desperation grip me again.

That is why I finally made an appointment, albeit several months later, to see the owner of the small shop I mentioned at the beginning of the chapter. Once again, my worst fears were realized. He had decided to close his shop. Guilt that my untimely action, or my later inaction, had contributed to the shop's closing nibbled at the edges of my conscience. I reminded myself that marketing isn't all that goes into a business. Many factors made the owner decide to close. The owner was positive about the mailings and our work together, which certainly helped. The decision to close was partly personal and partly the business climate for the shop. We parted on a friendly note, and I was personally glad for him that he was able to move on.

I have been able to move on, too, from allowing desperation to paralyze and limit my actions and my business. I did it through action.

Inaction feeds your fear of desperation and makes your fears become real. Action overcomes the paralysis of desperation and its effects. Action drives your business forward. The sooner you take action, the better for you and your business. If you find yourself feeling desperate, remember to take action immediately, even if you must force yourself to do so. Don't allow desperation to limit your business.

10
Communication: There's Never Enough.

Prior to starting my business, I worked for several corporations, every one of which experienced communication problems daily. I marveled at this communication quagmire, especially in the media corporations whose products were communications.

Then I started my own business.

Communication tripped me up

The first five years of my business, I noticed time after time how communication tripped me up. And *I* thought that I was quite savvy about communication. After all, not only was I a marketing consultant, but I had worked for several corporations in which lack of communication caused all kinds of problems. I thought that I had learned about communication from these corporate situations. While working for these corporations, at every position I took steps to improve communications. When I managed a retail store, I wrote and posted a weekly note that communicated to the employees the store's sales for the previous week, new items, and updated corporate information. During my employment at a radio station, I hired my own secretary to help me stay abreast of communications with both staff and customers. While a television sales representative, I always sent a note with schedule confirmations explaining to the customer in direct language what the confirmation covered. These confirmations were confusing to read because they were written in television jargon. Communication was *always* important to me.

But I came to appreciate an entirely new level of communication my first five years in business. Let me clarify to you what I mean by communication. I am referring to getting direct information about something to someone. I am not delving into the nuances of verbal vs nonverbal or using speaking styles or choice of one word over another in writing. Books have been written on these particulars, and I am not interested in getting that detailed about communication. My references to communication are the straightforward exchanges of information from one person to another. I am just amazed how demanding a clear exchange of information, or communication, can be.

Why is clear communication so difficult?

Busyness hampers communication.

In part it's due to the pace of our world. We all are so busy juggling so many different tasks at any given moment in both our personal and business lives that we don't pay attention to what we're being told. This is particularly true when you run a small business. You are wearing several hats, going from owner to worker to secretary to bookkeeper to janitor. Unlike large corporations, small businesses cannot afford the luxury of support personnel such as secretaries and janitors, and, therefore, the workload is distributed among fewer people. These people then, at any given moment, are juggling many different tasks because of their handling several positions. It's not surprising that they often don't comprehend all of what they are being told. At times, it's a wonder they comprehend any of it at all because of everything they are juggling at that moment.

Compound this busyness with a lack of listening skills, and you will begin to understand communication problems. Very few people have good listening skills. Why? Listening skills are learned, and most of us are too busy talking to learn to listen. I know because I've been there. To listen, you must consciously make yourself stop talking, ask the person an open-ended question, and then force yourself to focus on the person's response. You cannot allow your listening to be disrupted by thinking of your own response while the other person is talking. You must think and respond to what the person says *after* the person finishes talking. If you don't, you will miss part of what the person says. You may even miss the entire point because small things can affect the meaning of a statement.

I learned to listen when I started selling. There's a classic phrase in selling that states you can talk yourself out of a sale. This means you didn't listen to the customer, and therefore, when the customer was ready to buy, you kept talking and either annoyed the customer or said something that made the customer change his or her mind. I made this mistake one of my first days in selling radio. During my sales call, the lady who owned a waste hauling business that had not been on the radio for a long time decided to buy a schedule. I was so excited about the sale that I kept right on talking, and she changed her mind. Not only did my talking lose the sale, but, more importantly, I'm certain that I hadn't listened to her either.

Listening is active.

You see, listening is an active, not a passive, activity. Most people don't listen partly because they think it's boring and partly because what someone else says often triggers thoughts in their minds. They either want to express these thoughts immediately, or the thoughts lead their minds away from focusing on the conversation. To listen well, you must rein in your mind from drifting away on tangents that are triggered by what someone else is saying. This takes conscious, deliberate effort and training. Few school themselves to do this, and that's why people don't listen.

Beyond listening, inattention to communication on the part of the communicator is a third contributor to lack of communication. In other words, for whatever reason, you didn't tell what you thought you had told. Although this sounds negligent, it is easy to have happen. Usually, it is not deliberate. You simply think they know. You think somehow you *did* tell them. And maybe you did. Maybe they didn't listen. Or, maybe they had their minds on something else at the time.

Or, maybe you really *didn't* tell them.

It's impossible to prove what caused a communication problem. In the long run, it doesn't matter. All that does matter is that you communicate clearly. All that does matter is that your clients and your employees know the information they need to know. All that does matter is that you know that they *understand* the message.

Communicate often and repetitively.

To achieve this, you must communicate often and repetitively. Never assume that you told them, or that they heard you. You can't teach people to listen, and you can't change the pace of their lives to keep their minds focused on your message. You can, however, reiterate your communication several times and in several ways. Use speaking, writing, e-mail, drawing, or whatever methods you have available to get the message across.

And keep people informed about your work as it progresses. Although you have been busy behind the scenes doing a great deal for the client, it is important to keep the client informed of your actions. While you're thinking that you're working hard, the client has no way of knowing this unless you tell him. Tell him everything, not just the big things. Tell him the all important details that make your work valuable to him.

I take on a job and dive into it full force. In my absorption of getting the work completed, I can neglect telling the client what is happening. More than once, I thought I had told my client enough information on what I was doing only to discover that I would have been wiser to have told more. Now, you may say that a client either doesn't want or need to know everything about your work for him or her, but I challenge you to tell the client too much. If you find your client saying, "I don't want to know that," please let me know, because I have not yet found that situation.

Usually the little things that didn't get communicated are the problems.

Tell the little things.

Those little things turn into big things if not communicated. Sometimes the little things are not under your control. I had a printing company who had delays because of paper not being shipped or presses not functioning or personnel getting injured. I've run into problems because my computer went down. I've had problems with one project's eating up time that was to be used toward another project. There are many little things that can affect the flow and timeliness of a project.

Through it all, it's important to keep the client informed. Tell him or her of a delay, and tell as soon as possible. Tell the sequence of your work so that he or she understands not only what you are doing but also the flow of your work. Tell suggestions and problems immediately. The better informed your client is, the better your relationship will be, and the more he or she will value your work.

When I have neglected to tell my client immediately of a delay, a problem, or a change, inevitably the client called me, and I was placed in the uncomfortable position of explaining rather than the proactive position of informing. The information remains the same, it's just that the positions have changed. The best defense is a good offense in communication as well as in sports. Proactive communication strengthens your position with the client whereas explanations after the fact leave seeds of doubt, not only about your communications, but perhaps also about your integrity and even your work.

Communication saves you hassle with your client. Communication also increases your value to the client.

Communication increases your value.

When you tell your client the extras you have done and when you make your client aware of just what has gone into your work, you become more valuable to your client. I have a habit of getting something completed and not communicating what went into that completion. This lack of communication has always hurt me in the long run because I made what I had done look too easy. Why did it look easy? I didn't communicate what I had done to accomplish the task.

Now you may be thinking, "What's wrong with that? Isn't your goal to complete the task?" Yes, it is. However, when your client or your boss, doesn't know what went into completing the task, he or she does not understand what you have done for them. Without that understanding, he or she cannot fully appreciate your work. And without that appreciation, he or she cannot value you and your work appropriately. This undervaluing is not the fault of your client. It is your fault for not communicating to him or her what you have done. It's difficult for anyone to appreciate something of which he or she is unaware.

As with any lesson, communication is not one you learn and chalk up to experience. Communication is a lesson you practice every day, or you feel the sting of not communicating. It seems no matter how vigilant that I think I am in communicating, I still run into situations in which I do not communicate.

However, in retrospect, I can tell that I did not communicate well. It's interesting how 20-20 hindsight reveals a lack of communication, isn't it? I'm amazed that I can see it later, but not at the time.

Use foresight in your communications. Communicate early and often. Communicate today. Don't put off communicating changes, delays, or problems. Communication: There's never enough.

11
Follow-up: The Key to Peace and Prosperity.

One of my first clients cautioned me never to trust anyone to get something done correctly always and to check up on everyone. After years of handling his own advertising, he maintained that if you placed an ad, in whatever the media, it was wise to follow up and make certain that the ad had been placed and placed correctly. Further, check to see that your instructions had been followed. At the time I thought that this was a very cynical way to view the world, but I discovered that it was a very realistic view.

Following his suggestion, albeit borderline instruction, I contacted the media in which I had placed his ad and discovered problems. I was amazed. I couldn't believe that media could get it so wrong and not check to see if what they had was correct or not. After I corrected the problem, I became very paranoid and rechecked to see that the correction had been processed. Even then, there were problems. This shocked me. I still cannot believe how it can be so wrong and no one checks.

People are not doing this deliberately. Still, it is happening. And because they are not deliberately doing it, they do not see a need to check up on it. In fact, knowing the amount of times that I have followed up and found problems over the years, it sometimes amazes me that *anything* happens correctly.

Now *I* sound cynical.

Think through projects.

I am not singling out the media as the only companies at which things go wrong and are not followed up. Mistakes and lack of follow-up are everywhere. I believe the reasons that these mistakes and lack of follow-up happen are all wrapped up in our busy lifestyles. We tend not to focus on a project closely enough to see if all the details are handled. We tend not to focus on a project long enough to think through the potential problems that may happen as the project goes through its various stages and different hands. We tend not to focus on a project in a timely fashion so that we can check for errors before it is too late. We are so busy keeping several balls in the air and multi-tasking that we don't give individual projects enough attention, and, therefore, mistakes happen. We focus on quantity over quality.

The printing industry has faced this dilemma increasingly as time crunches demand work be done yesterday. In addition, desktop publishing gives the impression that "anyone" can create pieces to be printed. With training, anyone *can* create his or her own print pieces. Unfortunately, many people dive into software publishing programs and create pieces to be printed without knowing how printers want pieces submitted to them. Usually, these people lack training in the use of type or layout. Hence, printers get pieces on disk that they cannot open or that are in a software program from which the printer cannot go to press.

In most instances, these people want the pieces printed yesterday.

The printer now must take extra time to go over the piece, possibly recreate it himself, and ready it for printing. What is so difficult about that, you say? Well, if each change, and I mean every change, is not checked and rechecked with the client, the final printed piece may be incorrect. And every change made increases the likelihood of creating a problem or missing a correction. It is amazing how a small detail can make a big difference.

Check and recheck.

Even after all this checking and rechecking, upon viewing the completed piece, the client may change his or her mind on how something was worded or wish that something else would have been included. All of this comes from not thinking through the piece before it was presented to the printer.

In addition, a client's ignorance of the printing industry causes the client to give the printer pieces in an unusable form. Most clients are not aware they are making this mistake until the printer informs them. When I started my business, I did not know the printing industry nearly as well as I know it now. I have been fortunate along the way to work with a printing company that has been very helpful to my learning about the industry. My follow-up lessons were emphasized every time I had a piece printed. Every time that I did *not* recheck a piece, I later always found something wrong. Had I rechecked the piece, I probably would have caught the error. In one instance, I changed a part of the piece and sent the correction directly to the prepress company instead of through the printer. The prepress company sent the file back to the printing company, and because I thought everything was set, I did not recheck the proof. I believed that the prepress company had inserted the correction into the publication.

They had not.

When I saw the final publication, the original, not the correction, had been printed in the publication. Since I had sent the correction directly to the prepress company, the printer had never seen the correction. Therefore, the printer did not know that there was an error. The prepress company had not double-checked the change, and, obviously, neither had I.

Reprinting the corrected publication was not an option because it would be too expensive. Hence the correction never did appear in the publication.

So who was to blame?

Blame doesn't matter.

In a situation like this, and in any follow-up situation, when you get to the point of placing blame, it is too late. Blame won't change the outcome. Blame won't change the fact that the correction was not in the publication.

In our society, we are quick to place blame and not to accept responsibility for our actions. In this situation, I accepted responsibility for not following up on the change that I had given to the prepress firm. I assumed, which always gets me in trouble, that everything was all set. I assumed that there was nothing that could go wrong. I didn't stop to think about the change and the possibility that the change would not be made. The printer also felt responsible. However, there was no way for the printer to have known whether the correction was in the publication or not because the printer had not been aware of the correction. The prepress company did not accept *any* responsibility for the situation. I never asked why. I assumed that the company felt that following up to insure that a correction had been inserted into the publication was not its responsibility.

Does this matter? Well, the prepress's refusal to accept any responsibility certainly affected the prepress company's reputation with me and, perhaps, with the printer. Whether you are responsible or not, accepting at least part of the responsibility for a situation makes you bigger and better than refusing to accept any at all.

To assure the best outcome, take a proactive

approach with follow-up, follow-up, follow-up, so that you do not have to address an unpleasant situation. You don't want to be in a situation in which blame is an issue. While it can be useful to learn from your mistakes as to why a situation happened, at that point a situation has been created that cannot be changed. Or, if it could be changed, it would be costly to do so. It is much less stressful to follow up relentlessly, and perhaps too frequently, than to be distressed over a situation that could have been avoided with follow-up.

Practice follow-up.

Follow-up is not just applicable to individual projects but also to clients. To truly serve your clients, proactive follow-up must be your mantra. What are your clients' current situation? What is new with your clients? What are their current problems? How do they feel about your work? Don't wait for clients to call you. Proactively contact them. Keep in touch. Be on top of their situations so that you can be there to serve them in a timely manner, and that is before, not after, they need your services. Initiate follow-up to maintain your clients' business.

Do the same with your employees and the professionals with whom you work. Set the parameters within which they are to work. Set the follow-up meetings or reports. Then make sure these meetings or reports happen. Always expect to do the follow-up. Never expect someone else to do it. When a task hasn't been done correctly, don't be disappointed. Anticipate problems before they happen. Be pleasantly surprised when a task is performed correctly. This attitude greatly reduces stress and frustration.

I learned not to be disappointed in lack of follow-up when I was president of the Western Wisconsin Ad Club. We would send out meeting notices and request RSVPs. Before every meeting, the same half dozen people would religiously call in their RSVPs. The other eighty-four would need to be called, which I did. Several Ad Club board members felt that these calls were unnecessary. They claimed that members "should be adults and not need to be babysat with reminder calls." That is all well and good in theory, but in real life, it does not work. Following up with calls encouraged members to attend meetings and let them know that their participation was important to the group. Although it took time, I enjoyed these calls and, as a consequence of the calls, became better acquainted with the members. Eventually pressure from the board stopped me from doing the calls, and no one else did them either. The result was a rapid decline in attendance at the meetings.

Follow-up's lesson: You get out of something what you put into it.

Invest time and energy in follow-up.

When you invest the time and energy to follow up in any situation, the quality of the situation's outcome rises dramatically. The old adage that you get what you pay for is certainly applicable to follow-up. In many instances you are paying the price in thinking, time, and energy rather than in money. Your result, however, is more than just having a correct outcome. Your result also includes a lack of stress, a lack of wasted time, and a lack of emotional output applied to correcting a problem.

If you've ever tried to get a quote from a company to repair or remodel your home or apartment and not even received a return call, you can understand the stress, wasted time, and emotional output involved in the lack of follow-up. And that's just on one side, the customer's. You, as a business person, also experience more stress, wasted time, and emotional output when you lack follow-up. These affect your business and your personal life. Instead of proactively seeking new business, you are mired in cleaning up problems that could have been avoided by follow-up.

Follow up. Follow up relentlessly. Remind yourself to follow up today. Remind yourself to follow up tomorrow. Follow up every day and in every situation. Follow up, even when you are not responsible. Follow-up reduces stress and proactively seeks new business. Follow-up will bring peace and prosperity to your life.

12
Committees Have One Too Many Bosses

It's difficult to work for a committee.

Why?

By definition, each member of a committee is a decision-maker. Each member of that committee legitimately has input into the end product. Each member of that committee has his or her own ideas of what the end product should be. Each member of that committee comes with his or her own paradigms. The contribution of each member to the whole makes it very difficult to arrive at a consensus. Every individual client may have difficulty making decisions, may change his or her mind, may carry personal agendas, may not communicate well, and may not be satisfied easily. With committees, these potential pitfalls of dealing with one client are not only multiplied but, due to the interaction of the various committee members with each other, also magnified.

More people to satisfy.

When you have more than one person to satisfy, it's more likely that someone on the committee may not be satisfied with the end result. At that point, your problems depend on the dissatisfied person's strength on the committee. Does the dissatisfied member's opinion carry a great deal of weight? Does the dissatisfied member persist until the committee succumbs to that member's wishes?

I worked for one committee whose members, for the most part, were not nasty or aggressive. However, one member was very much that way. Unfortunately, this member was quite dissatisfied with my work and, at the end of the job, suggested to the committee that they not pay me for my services. The rest of the committee felt this was unfair, but since this member was so aggressive and would not back down on the stance of at least paying me less than the agreement stated, the committee sent me a reduced payment. They made this decision without discussing the action with me. My knowledge of the reduced payment came upon my receipt of the check, which included a note as to their decision. Had I been working with one decision-maker, I probably would have known of that person's dissatisfaction as the project progressed and been able to satisfy him or her prior to my being paid. With a committee, I did not know how each member felt and, consequently, was not able to take care of the problem and satisfy the customer as I would have with an individual decision-maker.

Can you keep in touch with a committee?

To keep individuals satisfied, you need to keep in touch with them. Keeping in touch with each member of a committee requires a great deal of time and effort and, in reality, probably won't happen. Just think about some of the normal problems of communicating with one person: trying to reach him or her, checking that he or she understands what you are saying, and getting information to him or her in a timely manner. Now multiply those problems times the number of people on a committee, and you begin to get an idea of the enormous communication problems which may develop.

I learned this the hard way. On the first face-to-face meeting to discuss a project with one of my clients, I found that the client had invited three additional people to attend. These people were introduced as "helping" the client with this project. I had thought that I would be reporting directly to the client, but, as the project developed, every contact with the client was communicated to the other three individuals, too. The client preferred that I report via e-mail, which promptly was forwarded to the other three individuals. These individuals, upon receipt of the e-mail, felt prompted to respond in some way to the e-mail by giving their opinions or asking questions. Not only did this result in several e-mail responses to which I then had to reply, but it also triggered additional phone calls. All this was very time-consuming.

Committees change decisions.

It also changed the decisions. When one individual is setting the parameters for a project, the parameters can be set and, although they may be subject to slight changes, will probably remain the same throughout the project. (Unless the decision-maker has difficulty making decisions-which is another subject altogether. For our purposes, we'll assume the decision-maker *can* make a decision and feels comfortable in doing so.) Now factor into the equation several people contributing to the decision, each with his or her own ideas of what the decision should be and each wanting to make a contribution to the project. What do you have? You have delays in making decisions. You have changes in guidelines as to how decisions are made. You have a confusing situation.

Here's what happens. Each decision is thoroughly reviewed by all committee members and may be subject to different lines of thinking from previous decisions, depending on which member of the committee is most forceful in stating his or her case of what the decision on that part of the project should be. Therefore, as the project progresses, the rules may change, depending on the dominance of any particular member at any given time. The rules may change not just once, but several times. They may bounce around, a rule being effective today and not tomorrow but, then again, applicable next week. It all depends on which individual and, consequently, which thinking is dominant at the time.

Rules may fluctuate.

Now you may be thinking, "Committees are not that disorganized. They will decide on a course of action and stick with it." This may be so at times. I have found it to be more likely that rules are subject to fluctuation and, even worse, that committee decisions can be *un*decided.

Yes, I mean that the rules are rethought, reversed, changed, or altogether undone. The rules are stuck in a committee quagmire.

One of my first clients was a committee. Although I worked with the person in charge of marketing for the company, several executives also had input into the final decision. The result was a stagnant situation that went nowhere. I made several suggestions to them on improving their marketing, all of which were interesting to some, but not to all, and subsequently never used. Finally, in frustration, I gave them a presentation which walked through on a basic level where their marketing was and where it needed to be. That, too, resulted in *no* action. Mercifully for me and unfortunately for my successor, they hired someone else to handle their marketing. Later, in talking to firms who had previously helped them with their marketing, I found this indecision to be a pattern with this firm. This pattern was due to a committee's making decisions and having difficulty doing so.

This is the most frustrating part of working for a committee. It can be extremely difficult to get a final decision. Preliminary decisions as to whether or not to proceed on investigating a project can be relatively easy to achieve, but finalizing a project can be excruciating. Here again, each individual member's desire to contribute and all members' differing opinions may stymie the decision.

Personal agendas affect your work.

Each member comes with his or her own personal agenda. This agenda may include how he or she wants to affect the results of the committee. For example, if a situation arises that reminds a committee member of a similar situation that he or she has encountered, it will trigger a response from the prior situation. Remember the situation I cited earlier of the committee member who was dissatisfied with my work? I believe that member had his own personal agenda because he had been doing some of the work that I was hired to do. That member had a particular idea of what needed to be done and how it should be done. He was not open to new ideas.

A personal agenda may not have any specificity attached. It may simply be a personal agenda which is unrelated to the specific workings of the committee. It may be baggage that an individual member brings to his or her involvement in the committee. A personal agenda, however unrelated to the specific committee, may have a disruptive impact on the workings of the committee.

I encountered a situation in which a personal agenda cost me a great deal of time, money, and frustration. This personal agenda involved the details of the text of a brochure for which I was creating the layout. When I say details, I mean details. For example, should the time be typed as 9 a.m. or 9:00 a.m.? Could factual information be abbreviated with a period following, or did all information need to be presented in full, grammatically correct sentences? Should the hours be stated as "Open 9 a.m.-5 p.m."? Or, should a full sentence be used, such as "XYZ Company is open 9 a.m. to 5 p.m."? Should zip codes be included in the addresses? Each person who proofed the layout had his or her own personal agenda on what these details should be. Each time the piece was proofed, which was at least five, details that had not been addressed before would be changed. If this had been a basic brochure, these changes would only have been an annoyance, but since this was a multiple page brochure, each detail change had to be applied to the entire book. When detail changes are made to a book after it has been laid out, some changes are easily missed. Consequently, the final result has a greater likelihood of errors than if the details had not been changed. Plus, it is very costly in time and money to make these changes. Add into the mix the frustration of addressing details five times, and you can begin to understand the effect this project had on me and my business.

I learned from this experience to avoid working with committees, if at all possible.

How to work with committees.

If you feel that you want to work with a committee, follow these suggestions that I learned from my mistakes in working with committees. While it's important to clarify all aspects of your working relationship from the onset with every client, it's even more important with committees. Establish objectives and parameters of work clearly in your agreement. Agree on a time frame in which decisions must be made. Include time lines for the final decision and also timelines for minor decisions. These minor decisions, if not made, will hold up the entire project. Set up how, when, and with whom communications will be carried out. Ask to be kept informed of the committee's opinions, individually and collectively, of your work. If you clearly outline your working arrangement with a committee prior to starting work, you *may* be able to minimize some of the pitfalls of indecision, changing of minds, personal agendas, faulty communication, and dissatisfaction. I don't believe that you can eliminate them completely because of the nature of the committee beast. Whenever you have several people who have input into a project, the pitfalls to achieving that project are multiplied.

Work with committees if you want to, or must, but do so with your eyes wide open and take steps up front to minimize potential problems. Plan in advance for these problems; acknowledge them when they arise; and tackle them immediately. There are as many reasons not to work with committees as they have members. Hence, if you work with committees, remember that you are dealing both with individuals and with the group dynamic that these individuals create. Committees have one too many bosses, each with their own agenda.

13
Frustration Is an Energizing Force

About five years into my business, I hit a wall of pure frustration. I was frustrated with some of my clients. I was frustrated with my income. I was frustrated with the direction of my business.

"Success Teams" accomplish dreams.

Luckily, around this time I became involved in a "Success Team." This is a team of four to eight people who meet on a weekly basis initially to define goals and then to help each other accomplish those goals. Our team started with six people. The success team concept is from Barbara Sher, author of Wishcraft. Barbara's premise is that it is very difficult to accomplish goals alone, but with others holding you accountable, giving you input, and encouraging you through the rough times, you can accomplish your dreams. You can dream bigger dreams and accomplish them, too.

When I joined the success team, I was president of the organization that was sponsoring the team, Wisconsin Women Entrepreneurs-Chippewa Valley Chapter. I felt in my role as president that I should be a team player and join the first success team, particularly if there weren't enough people to start the team. I didn't feel that the success team would do anything for me.

Was I wrong.

A few weeks into the series, Barbara has a lesson

in expressing frustration. She calls it "Hard Times." Barbara recommends that you have a session of expressing to another person your frustration, fear, anger, or any other negative feeling that you have been keeping bottled up inside yourself. Ask the person to sit and listen while you rant and rave about the negative feelings that you are experiencing.

Well, I thought this was a foolish, ineffective lesson, but not wanting to go to the success team meeting and admit to not doing the lesson, I asked a friend to listen while I expressed my frustration. Wow! Once I started, my expression of frustration crescendoed to a degree that shocked even me. I didn't know how frustrated and angry I was at my current business situation.

I felt caught in a trap of doing a great deal of work, not making enough money, and running around in circles. I was drifting away from my core business. I was dealing with some situations and people at the time that added to my frustration. All of these pent up feelings came pouring out that morning.

Thank you, Barbara.

During our success team meeting, I told what had happened to me in my "Hard Times" session. I found more anger and frustration come bubbling to the surface as I recounted my story. Then my fellow success team participants began to tell me and to help me see how I had put myself in this frustrating situation by my actions. By agreeing to work with the people with whom I was working, by accepting the projects on which I was working, by being willing to work for the amount of money for which I was working, and by accepting the payment conditions under which I was working, I alone was responsible for placing myself in my situation. I had no one to blame but myself for my frustration.

And I was the only one who could do anything about it.

What did I *do*?

I discovered that after our success team meeting ended, I began to feel more and more energized. I mulled over my outburst of frustration for several days. I thought about what my success team members had said. They told me that I had allowed, even created, this situation. Had I? After much thought, I reluctantly admitted to myself that I had done so. Only *I* could change the situation. It was up to me.

I considered what actions I must take to change my situation.

Value yourself first.

First, I realized that I needed to value myself and my work more than I had been doing. How could I expect others to value me and my work at the level that I wanted if I did not first do so myself? So I had discussions with myself. And I do mean discussions, plural. I did a great deal of soul-searching to discover why I didn't value myself subconsciously at the level that I wanted the world to value me. From this, I began to understand my insecurities which were the foundation of my poor value of myself. All were fear-based: fear of not getting work, fear of not getting the work done well, fear of not having the work completed on time, and, ultimately, fear of not maintaining my business. I have since discovered that these are the typical fears that entrepreneurs face.

How did I face these fears? I listened to tapes from Nightingale Conant and read several books that gave me positive instructions on how to handle these fears. More importantly, I acted on the helpful suggestions that I had read and heard. I looked differently at myself. When I caught myself being fearful or questioning my value, I stopped, had a talk with myself, and inserted into my mind positive thoughts about my value. Could I stop these negative thoughts? No. But I was successful in apprehending them. I was constantly vigilant in monitoring my thoughts. As I did so, I slowly improved my value of myself in my mind.

This was the first step in addressing my frustration.

Decide on a goal.

Next, as I felt more valuable, I took a good look at the business that I was doing. Were the activities and the clients with whom I was dealing getting me toward my goals? In general, the answer was no. I realized that doing what I had been doing was making some money but not driving me forward toward my goals. I was taking projects to survive. I was doing the comfortable projects. I had not written my goals on paper and decided on a course to achieve them. That made it quite easy for me to just follow any path. The adage, "If you don't know where you are going, any road will get you there," was quite applicable to my situation. I was ambling down any old path which offered money. I wasn't choosing the path I wanted to travel. I was out of control.

I decided on some short-term goals, and I took action on them. My first goal was to extract myself from working with current situations which were unprofitable and featured frustrating people. This was not accomplished overnight. First, agreements had to be fulfilled, which I did. Then receivables had to be collected, which took a little longer. Finally, I had to back away from these situations by either outright nonrenewal of agreements, or I had to fade away from the situation through deliberate noncontact.

As I was working through this extrication process, as well as after it, I resolved not to take on frustrating people or situations again if I could help it. So I made a list of "rules" to help myself avoid these situations.

My rule list is as follows:

Do not work with committees.

Work with situations that have only one person who makes the decision rather than deal with a manager and a general manager, both of whom may have input into the decision.

Work with people who can and do make decisions.

Treat all friends as I would strangers in business dealings.

Listen to my "gut feelings." If a situation doesn't feel right, don't do it.

Always have an agreement signed before I begin work.

Price the project fairly for myself and for the client.

Do not "give away" ideas to clients to get their work. Ideas are what I have to sell. If I give them away, I have nothing to sell.

Value myself and my work at the level that I want others to value me.

Since then, I have lived by these rules. At times I have broken them, always to my regret. Sometimes I have discovered that a situation was not what I had thought it was, such as a one decision-maker situation turning into a committee, and I have extricated myself as quickly and as cleanly as possible. I still have discussions with myself as to my value, which I suspect I will continue to do. If I adhere to these rules, my business and my life have far fewer frustrations.

Having the patience to work through this frustration and pulling myself to where I wanted to be rather than slipping back to where I had been were challenging, and continue to be so. This has been a process, a process that has taken months, not days or weeks. It's a process I am still working, parts of which I will continue to work. It has not been easy, but I have found in following this process a freedom to pursue my dreams. Although frustration often gets very bad press and is something most people try to ignore, I have found frustration to be a friend, a friend alerting me to my dissatisfaction.

When you feel frustration, listen to it. Frustration is an energizing force knocking at your mental and emotional doors. Grab it by the hand, work through it, and on the other side of frustration, you will find an energy and a freedom you cannot anticipate.

14
Mistakes: An Attitude of Gratitude

This book has deliberately focused on my mistakes in hopes that you will learn from them. I am grateful for my mistakes.

Why?

My mistakes have enabled me to learn, albeit the hard way, how to conduct my business and myself in a winning fashion. They have helped me to build a profitable business. As I have read and heard in the past and was recently reminded of again in Robert Kiyosaki's works, winning comes from losing. Handling your business profitably comes from making mistakes and learning from them.

My hope in writing this book and sharing my mistakes with you is that I can help you learn from your mistakes. Or, perhaps I can help you avoid making some mistakes. However, I would not wish that you do not make any mistakes because it is from making mistakes that you will learn your most valuable lessons.

Be grateful for your mistakes.

So embrace your mistakes. Be grateful for them. Take them by the hand and get to know them. Find out why and how they happened. Then make changes so that you do not encounter them again.

Seek advice from books, tapes, seminars, and professionals on how to stop making mistakes and how to avoid making them at all. Let your mistakes lead you to a team of professionals such as bookkeepers, accountants, attorneys and consultants who can help you avoid future mistakes and can help your business grow stronger and faster than if you had not enlisted their services.

Keep learning. Never stop. It is what makes life interesting. It is what will keep you interested in your business.

And keep making mistakes. Just be sure they are new mistakes. Making mistakes is not bad; making the same mistakes over and over again is. Making mistakes, if you learn from them, is the way to grow. It is the way of the winner.

As I finish writing about the mistakes I made my first five years in business, I wonder what mistakes I will make the next five years. I'm curious to discover them. Before they even arrive, I'm grateful that I will have an opportunity to experience and to learn from them.

Index

About the Author

Elizabeth K. Fischer owns Profitable Sales and Marketing Consultants, a marketing consulting company which helps small businesses by innovative marketing. In addition, Profitable Sales and Marketing Consultants is involved in selling and distributing Midwest Notebook, a TV feature series on tourism in the Midwest which is now streaming video online and creating an online portal for Midwestern tourism.

A past president of the Western Wisconsin Ad Club and a speaker at marketing workshops, she is continually seeking the most profitable ways for small businesses to reach their markets. Her first book, Mistakes I Made My First 5 Years in Business (and How You Can Avoid Them), will be followed by two upcoming books What's in It for Me? Marketing from a Customer's Point of View and Mistakes I' Made Buying Advertising.

About the cover designer and editor

Jill Olsen, cover designer, may be reached at jolsentype@aol.com.

Sharon R. Lowry, editor, may be reached at sharon@psmc.com.

About the printer

Badgerland Printing, printer, may be reached at badgerprinting@aol.com.

Share <u>Mistakes I made My First Five Years in Business (and How You Can Avoid Them.)</u> with your friends and colleagues.

Order on-line at mistakesImade.com, www.monarchtreepublishing.com, or amazon.com.

For information, please contact:
Monarch Tree Publishing,
P. O. Box 387
Eau Claire, Wisconsin 54702-0387
(888) 895-7166
Fax: (715) 874-6766
info@www.monarchtreepublishing.com
www.monarchtreepublishing.com

To be released in 2003:
What's in It for Me? Marketing from the Customer's Point of View
Mistakes I Made Buying Advertising
Order your advance copies on-line at www.monarchtreepublishing.com.